Plainspeak
Astrid Alben

( ) (   )   p   prototype

prototype publishing
71 oriel road
london e9 5sg
uk

Design by Zigmunds Lapsa

Typeset in Lelo (Camelot Typefaces)

Printed in the UK by TJ International

A CIP record for this book is available
from the British Library

ISBN: 978-1-9160520-2-4

( )   (   )   p   prototype

(type 1 // poetry)

www.prototypepublishing.co.uk
@prototypepubs

Contents

'It means exactly what I've said, literally and completely, in all respects.'

– Arthur Rimbaud

'I have made this drawing several times – never remembering that
I had made it before – and not knowing where the idea came from.'

– Georgia O'Keeffe

Plainspeak

Plainspeak

Just before dawn stars pause above us. Space is
photogenic. Oxygen uranium & gold Poet is what we

are made of. One life is not enough to run breathe run
run Poet run across the autobahn orbiting Earth no

need for pausing for cameras blaze a trail grinning
from me to yours burst open speak plainspeak

Oh Poet I love you Poet if no one else will love you Poet
without you I am shadowless the naked part of canvas.

Collateral Damage

Poet hadn't yet made Earth the jobless vigorously typed
not yet news bulletins absolutes weren't yet accident prone

lunatics all wore the same garments no one cockgobbled
a shame not yet sodomites thought love declarations were

daylight saving lies coughed politely from the wings. Words
standing still before Poet stood still a harelipped giant bowing

his head before the mountain in so doing paid homage
to the mountain patiently rivers down its sides.

Vodka & Lime

High up in atmosphere, vertigo intact inside vodka & lime
stashed lifejacket under front seat checked foot underneath

me spins planet Earth. Oil rigs, tankers, pleasure craft, that
accident in 1995 resulted in my crooked smile thin strip of coast

estuaries see those legolicious houses — if I had a big house big
enough to fit I'd have to leave because there'd be no room for me

I could easily fly like this a long long time but the captain won't
tell won't tell he won't tell I yell where my wings are.

Hermaphrodite

Shape of a screaming Goya face-to-face with the face of
my early life a boy is a boy by birth not a girl not a choice is

breaking news worse far worse than when Poet longed to grow
up a Jew chronicle man's history hard-pressed to my diasporic

chest. A slug (hermaphrodite) glides from B to trachea
drainpipe go-kart boy girl girl boy boy girl girl Goya boyohboy

Goy — the rage of sex is fragile outlives the scattered ruins
no amount of Fairy Liquid will wash the mucus off.

The First People
for Marlene Dumas

Your credibility is shot through the opposite
beautiful smearkisses on every bit of I'm asleep

to the question *are you asleep* or *no awake* to the same
lullaby then asks incredulously *really awake?*

Rudderless coochy coo tumbles through a bottomless
process like colony collapse everything rotting

dehydrating & disintegrating decomposes the universe
no end a colossal baby trying to climb out of its cunt.

Herky Jerky

Elevator up & down the generations rocks a dinosaur
shifts mountain lakes iron ore its weight from left to right

I'm a sudden coolness in the air I'm coming down
rain — the kind the eye can see like Poet playing air guitar

and love home envy kitchen table a complex of occasions is
my mother playing solitaire. She listens to the radio.

She's not there she's up she's down shifts her chair
will crash into Earth thirty billion years from now.

Coping Strategies

Poet takes some après-ski delight in the departure lounge
beyond his reflection tarmac his suitcase on a baggage trailer I

see he packed shoelaces camouflage. Backup. Indistinctly one
origami swan gathers up its quills accelerates on the runway _transformation_

halfway announces shutters down for take off behind a decorative
fern a television honks its head off: information a non-local

quantity. Ink *every*where. Skidding would be catastrophic Poet
observes cautiously lost cohesion. Better flight before light.

Poet Seeks Travelling Companion

Poet at bus stop too has a monkey on my shoulder
doesn't have a monkey exactly how I imagined

the bus driver says two passengers. Poet sees only one
getting off the other getting on. Poet asks always driver

says longing & family fare. Poet asks how you tell which is
which driver says not my circus not my monkey.

Poet gets on. No.
Longing gets on.

Customs

I'm told to raise both arms. I raise both arms
phlegmatically in the way that hopes are dashed. Not a

single cell the same as seven years ago if every cell
renews itself how can it still be *stand still please* be me?

Certainties white lies a bottle of shampoo.
I stand naked like a Neolithic jar my body a refugee

burdened with anxious jealousy boarding pass fear
the examined life as short-lived tyranny.

Personal transformation, renewal + decay.

Self-reflection.

21

Conversation on Art

On *The Japanese Footbridge* by Monet I say the painter went
blind in old age

followed by a puzzled why in front of *Whistlejacket* strange
to paint a horse just be glad it's not a chicken why

walking across Marten's *Lunar Nibs* the difference between
the magical dumbness of objects & interpretation prop up

parallel worlds in front of a pyramid by Klee why it's either
free fall in a holdall through the gently gently why.

Getting There

Flight from Heathrow to Cork a nervous breakdown started
on the runway the female passenger next to me helped her

friend pass away yesterday. Aesea was conceived as the A-bomb
blazed a pre-ordained path through Hiroshima which is how she

died second-generation radiation as bad as dying instantly only
slower. We land. I lunch. Lie down. I masturbate to calm me

down. Like dying instantly, only slower. In Japan it's illegal
to be dead & in a grave. I hear flames chewing on the airwaves.

Terror in the Terminal

A backpack explodes a thousand times in Istanbul. Body
parts rain down like manna from a divine production

line. To the gods it's just another car alarm. A nude child
runs from barrier to sliding door a path it can't escape.

Only the eleventh time I click I see blood smears the walls
of arrival halls. Lean in takes a closer look. Press play.

Baggage claim stands exactly where it stood this running
child never grows tired as inset left gods retake their aim.

Komodo Dragons at London Zoo

[handwritten annotation: Puns + semantic zeugma between enjambed lines + stanzas.]

Komodo dragons eat almost anything monkey rotten eggs
water buffalo fish they'll eat their own & pigs

like me they'll eat the contents of your fridge if they bite
your calf in half no calf. Yet in the Paleozoic

Komodos lived harmoniously huddled around open fires
fed on slow-cooked stews in terracotta pots their evolutionary

progress remained largely unexplained as baffling a phenomenon
as this low-frequency hum in desert air, Taos, New Mexico.

Poet in Need of a Wife

When a door opens or closes Poet can tell if that astronaut
is in orbit wears a paperclip in his thinning hair

when he talks to the philatelist he weighs his misery in Kafkas
when to blabbermouth his livestock is counted in copyright

when he talks to Camille Claudel it's in Bahia de bahia
with his feather boa constrictor & punctuation crumbs

to the Kronos Quartet Poet will sing about jazz in sexiness
while the crowd applauds & applauds.

Stormy Night

Poet has been at his own throat for hours howled
the wrecking-balls from crab-apple trees and chased the

mutt indoors. Forepaws are thumpers. Tail now rests on
the 'OME' of the WELCOME mat the watchfulness of

an obscured pulse what twitches the hare
boxing the sped-up clouds through the night. The letterbox

chatters with tchs ohs wails & whys of last year's dead in
Poet's head. In my home filled with deafness only I'm awake.

reality is what you make of it — instead of worrying about lost subject objectivity, then, we should rejoice in our capacity to be free + remake the world)

Fugue for Wittgenstein

pun - can be whose shadow (is this) or (who is) this shadow?

The sound of someone who left the room as people
pass each other in Moscow corridors muttering

Da, but who's shadow? A planet orbiting without a universe
the astronaut who never makes it through the atmosphere

loneliness deliberate and slow love & desire that never
happened the hardest to let go — like Marlon Brando

mumbling through the best film ever made when
there are no questions left this itself is the answer.

*the world is its own thing
(language puts more steps between us + beauty
— but this is one neccesary step to encore
that beauty.*

Words To Say It

Washed-up language perplexed itself a squawking birdie
from the nest fall brainwaves crack & compromises Poet

alone stand. Haemorrhaging nouns the modal to its end
send. Whoa! Steady please! Lieber! Lieder! Lei—der

my mouth wend wi—der Dichter plunges capacity
expansion with his epileptic tonsil tickler pushes down

gender splendour soapsuds coursing through Poet's migrant
heart his utter udder other my spacetime ladder.

Putting It Back Together

Outside the wind overturns a bin plastic forks orange-tinted
paper God's gift to advertising Godzilla with

an amputated tail empty bag translucent waiting skin
a stranger's lips torn apart while best begin again plays

I found that book under chicken scraps pages flutter drunk
birdlike it can be roses what's mine shadows on a hot day

in April a hotel room just for the night and putting it all
back together that is that is

Déjà Vu

Poet has made this poem several times using blue Pelikan ink
then stopped remembering he made this before sits alongside

my peripheral vision in the way that particular toy I craved
as a child who has discovered the key of love I no longer see

what that was nevertheless was as important as the vanished link
between spontaneous utterance & the lapse of self lays down

the pen pushes back my chair whistles along Coolhurst Street
wearing bumper car shoes sucking on a hard boiled sweet.

Kafka's Contemplation

Two donkeys billy goat a windswept ewe & Kafka
determinedly schnozzled in clover marigold lichen

hawkweed milkwort Aster Pirri-pirri-bur Fool's Parsley
Shepherd's Purse. Kafka ruminates on dusk

tail swooshes construct a superhighway for bees & flies
light a tuning fork splits the best of friends in

silhouettes already here Palaeolithic beasts swarming
the horizon over my shoulder blade proliferate.

Nonfinito

Someone? thoughts roll into one another & become something else by their end.

Between the sanatorium & the playground ideas become
compromises comfort blankets joy divisions. Time discards

the beautiful it replaces — affection mother Antwerp Station
a leaking udder impossible arias that slug wet caress *muah*

Love

*Language
start,
to mirror
parody
futil*

muah betrays the one I never was in live's transmission.
Poet stares at the pre-evidence of the short-lived comical

accepted then rejected. Lazarus steps in *clapclapclapclapclap*.
Others say thinking.

*rhyme reads in
the possibility of
rhyme.*

Visiting a Pyramid

for Ingeborg Bachmann & Anselm Kiefer

[handwritten annotation: wonder + artistic creation are often smashed by time + the everyday.]

Your sleeping torso a pyramid weighs down your age
my age & the age of the world. Onlookers set up camp-style

folding chairs tune their binoculars on *sleep tight Poet* your
ruffled hair hieroglyphs spelling out the uprising across

an entire continent. Arms raised like windsocks as doodlebugs
sneeze into the desert settles in sheets. Come dawn tourists

wander through the wreckage taking shots while grave robbers
remove evidence with shopping lists behind the eyes.

Between the Lines

Poet reads your letter honestly more of a note.
At first Poet delighted

this gives me hope.
Hours wane hours roll over clouds

sink three-day hands in dishes
where bickering aristocrats wrestle Fairy Liquid

into a lake. At the lake's edge Poet overhears
his neighbour say *when it's quiet we can hear her read.*

Accidental Drowning *Anthropocene.*

Centuries-old fish scales, loaded alarm gun, radioactive toothpaste,
dentures, enema-syringes & 700,000 other archaeological finds

in construction pits expose joy & aghast consequentially plied in a way
miracles & mental breakdowns capsize life's eventualities. Mittelstand

Doktor Mengele had fingertip precision drowned with his inheritance
in perfect condition: a library stocked with Goethe, Goebbels,

Erich Fromm, Siegfried Lenz, medical lit. on soft-tissue rheumatism,
rollies, an Olympic souvenir placard, a packet of Olla brand condoms.

La Morte Amoureuse

Saito Ryokan said elegance is frigid he was right elegance
is a ballerina sinking in *plié*. Then Romeo killed whoever killed

Mercutio. Sarah Lamb better as a corpse than in a *pas de deux*
her body a second hand rootless rounds the clocks what did

this pair of star-crossed lovers plan to do sleep through death
pirouette their way to Veracruz in Mexico? Someone in the gods

coughs through Juliet's dying shifts. Poet looks up looks down
and to the left. The row to the left is looking at me.

Peeing in the Grass Along the River Ex

Voices hover on the river sweethearts kissing on the grass
the Romans were here. Dragonflies. Along the path a sign

for river roamers canoeists kids paddling the current like daisies
Danger / Electric Cables / Cross Canal Here / Keep Mid-Stream

I crouch among clover overlooking the cathedral sitting on
the city like a throne of abdicated kings

push my knickers to one side and as I pissed Poet thought
Cross Canal / I Thought / Cross Canal / Which Way

Scenic Route

Clouds under the car's roof nimbostratus mermaids
their fishtails slap the windscreen sheens a movie screen

showing slapstick comedy. Shorebirds glisten silver spoons
and a sky streaked like bacon. Oh lovely day away in dash marks

splitting the page in half clouds break apart salty popcorn
scatters the atmosphere and Poet in his herringbone

staring through the rolled-up
window readjusting his opinions neatly in the back.

Ripple Effect

In Exeter a boy plays football by himself in an oversized
blue-and-white striped anorak. It's mid-June.

Next door's dog is barking at the pond.
Soap bubbles that waft out above the trees are postcards

to the sun. They remind me of me craning my neck
at the invisible moorings of stars asking my father why moths

only come out at night yet are attracted by the light. Here
they are long before dusk over slow water.

good example of Plainspoke.

Many Things

He who resents the hungry mouth of public spaces should have
canoodled the library books he stole instead of boiling them that

night in a Le Creuset pot should have watered the hibiscus
before turning his attention to should have jumped then waited for

his body to catch up should have written his magnum opus
then burnt it in the bin should have stirred that pot if only to bring

summer back but if ever in one lifetime Poet is capable of many
deaths I should have waited for his body to catch up.

Radio Mast

How come sea turtles travel alone? Like satellites they have
faithfully shouldered their own frequency for one hundred million

years. Today is Sunday. Today is the boy I never got to be. He stands
before the radio mast *No!* he booms pushes out his ribs a woofer

Look! No! Me! face hands toes cling to the edge of dawn point
south of the border west of the sun. In GMT a night watchman

tunes his radio listens to the *WHHOOOOOOO* of the ocean
believes a sea turtle has just checked in to the Galaxy Hotel.

Je est un autre

      Arthur Rimbaud wrote.
There is another of the other. Poet hears 'I's an udder.'

You apparent ease monkey!   *Playful but informed.*
Onion of the union! Other! O—ther!

Either—eider! you or I. Both together out of the question!
I leave Poet in his own hectic majestic check into

the Grand Hôtel de l'Univers my udder skulking
flea-infested in the mirror over the four-poster bed.

Betrayal

The Prince Alfred on Castelmain Street covered in blood
in Brussels there's blood on your demands for peace skinny

girls outside the chippie covered in blood the sleazy rain
covered in blood the Porsche Spyder parked in a side street

this morning's headlines the awe-inspiring symmetry of
misery & all the wasters at the bar at lunchtime in the Prince

Alfred on Castelmain Street. Hows & whens tiptoeing away
en pointe covered in blood.

Nightreise

Intoxicated thumbs hooked to his belt hip swaying
Poet belches can't take that away upsadaisy reels away

which way can't say can't take that away.
Cars are nightly filed away horns sweetly snoring

hey! bear springs up in a jazzy curvet tussles Poet
by the epaulettes this & that a-way. Tuesday's miles away

and life a football pursued by a bear into the caboodle.
Poet & bear exit a disorderly affair kick the air.

In Conversation with David Hockney

What brings ya here Poet bellows through the trees
I muah muah kissing muah the air here *couldn't leave*

is loveness with or without light made for going the other
way *look!* he signals in semaphore *there!* on the right

another birch stripped purple of May. There now stands on
its own. Poet can place his thumbs forefingers about its

neck squeezing rarely forms the perfect shape amorphous
unchanging our schizoid hinterland billowing *every*where.

Morning Stretches

I raise these arms slowly isn't slow enough darkens
under the eyelids a car alarm goes off

an exhaust pops and the veins on the stock exchange
shoot up the grid then head down a bombed London

skyline hangs upside down with the sound down. I'm
upside down. Poet is exhausted. Day up. Day down.

Day up. Day down come evening says Schopenhauer
I will be poorer by a day.

Hallelujah

The old sun waltzes through August. Hail!
to be alive the heart steeped waist deep

in the persistent hum of ordinary days for years
I felt I should be somewhere else but not today

today I'm no stranger to trying to be human
in the empty stadium of life. Today (hallelujah)

today is nice. Emily, Ingeborg, Goya, Poet
I guess you too this is *mine mine mine* my *mine life.*

[handwritten annotation: Plain-speak means ...]

Flue & Fatigue

Sleep a drama junkie knocks on the eardrum BANG
the rhino hip-butts the whatnot & doodah a nocturne

pirouettes across the parquet floor an ostrich bolts
up the flue & fatigue of a desert caravan baroque paradoxes

stowaways & lorikeets hopping from page to fully automatic
intimacy Berryman, Emily, Poet & Goya too —

I open my mouth unable to form what lies ahead
a coming fear — a sleep that lasts for miles.

Oiseaux

When you call Poet listens to the message but won't return
the call I don't return the call when you clapeye Poet maudlin

at the bus stop kicking a puddle-stained flyer Poet won't
get on I don't get on when you invite Poet to your Thursday soirée

I say *yes all right*
instead Poet stays home like Lautréamont in a kimono hand

painted with turquoise amber coral blazing *oiseaux du paradis*
curtains drawn whistling poems I never heard before.

Emily Dickinson Disease

With loneliness too daily to relate Poet postpones absence
into words is taken off to a planet for his recovery signs

up to the Amateur Resistance Society instructs Poet how to bloom
through the Milky Way.

After lunch Poet sets off fades in a small lit up raft
laid to on an ocean of stars so weightless & vast

I'm left without you Poet with manoeuvres in *auf wiedersehen*
Poet with how come nothing means without you nothing Poet.

Seed or Spider

Poet discovers a seed dangling from a hair caught
between the top of two pages in *Collected Poems*

by James Schuyler. Either that or a shrivelled spider
'naked beside a black polluted stream'. Today

I have faith in the invisible fragility of time &
multiple division.

Poet is reading 'A Grave' which starts 'While we
who wished to help stood helplessly by'.

Poet in Need of a Rest

Come afternoon Poet walks shopping bags home then sun
overboard! takes shelter under the flyover cuts fingers puts

bags down inhales a grebe ducks under
the sun Poet sees standstill as camaraderie with the entanglement

of *time up* bobs the grebe elsewhere knuckles flex relax and
the daily grind grumbled in E Major is heard in endive batteries

& *oh hearty shame* Andrex toilet paper while the canal reflects
trucks & buses a mangy tennis ball hours *hours!* floating.

Waterloo Station

The clock is the size of the heart of a humpbacked whale
is a small planet an ace is you Shuffle! Let's play Stress

before the train is memory the reaction to how things
are is sixty-two miles to space — a four of clubs a queen

the knave — extend that ladder out of here forget the clock
its demented hands the whale the Pacific playing tricks on

our mind the conductor's whistle yelping String Quartet
No. 2 in F-sharp Minor on the platform Let go! Let go!

Five Ways of Belonging

I knock but the world is nowhere (one) to be found. Hail! to
the world! (two) anywhere under the weight of eiderdowns

a house sighs loneliness a half-completed line. Go to
the park (three) where gargoyle mouths on stilts (three & a half)

called bins count slender poplars in margins of the wind
riffling obsolescent papers, orange peels, Poet's insular

dominion masking tape I never (four) heard the voices near
the bench (five) cargo spaces blindly *bu-hu-woooshhh.*

Morning Papers

Poet squeezes his tiny head by its slot machines to quieten
the daily manslaughter, bedwetting, genital mutilation, lottery

results, pharma-corruption, a doomed giraffe upside down at
the rim of a cappuccino ring local flash floods coffee spoon

swirling the debris of thinking-out-louder *Idiocy! Ticket inspector!*
a heart crackling with violence & human kindness copulate

across pages ages no changes yes this is — gurgling deep
boisterous & road closures — what makes the ground mortal.

56

Venus

The only machine in the sky is the sun very bright
don't stare is bottomless as if clouds never were

Poet & I stare twosome then blindsome specks
bzzzzzzzzzing on our brow. Today I love you Poet

with your devoted crater eyes let's love each other
just the two of us apeman spaceman pick at scabs

by the galaxy's edge rest our heads on stars the sun
asleep in our sleep where fireflies explode.

Every Material

When you're finished reading can you turn off
the light? Poet lies puzzled up against my back

sleeping the light is out. Funny. Poet slips between
the cracks of the city behind the skyline of a flat

field disappears in the folds of the sheets between
the cracks of my fingers Poet requires a blind

woman's skill like the letter S smells of earth smells
of clay of long wires through short histories.

Road Kill

Poet drove through darkness a cat crossed the dyke.
I crouched it hissed goji berry from its tiny mouth wrestled

the shoulder blades from its spine to the moonless
night imploded on the ground. I carried the cat bundle-bride

to the damp grass lakeside Poet going kill it! Have mercy
the cat moaned end it *finit* me wring *mon petit cou* yet

I couldn't wring its neck headlights panting do the kinder
thing and keep tomorrow open strong.

Five Obstructions

I left the house a sleepwalker. I visited absurd places a newspaper
stand city buses aimlessly driving back & forth kids in headphones

a sea turtle in an underground car park listed all the books I read
by 2.42 a.m. Sleep won't come. Sometime always delayed doesn't

know where to begin and next the chaotic beauty of panic creeps
in the distance a heavy freight rolling through everything running

together pink orange violet the Alps glow-in-the-dark sea urchins
x-rays touch don't touch the world stops & starts with fireflies.

How Poet Hurt His Thumb

I can kill someone with kindness can answer that
question and *Oh be quiet* on my knees I'm electricity poles

in the snow on my way to Turkey *okay okay* these
imaginary tracks a tollgate swinging in & out

of focus wild beasts bleating happiness & helplessness
far in me I woke under a volcano howling inside I heard

Idiocy! Ticket inspector! that'll have been Poet
slammed it in the door and this is important not what door.

And Became a Monkey
for Hannah Höch

On tiptoe I follow God around his classroom as he
resumes his rebuttal of Poet's attributes — leniency

the persistent rumours he's cockalorum & the one where
we're nihilistic thoughts that come into his tra-la-la

hand in his pocket jangles a spectrum of promises most
memorable of which monkey-twitch is Poet's inside our

heads like a pinball machine with flippers going balls
knocking the bumpers playing I don't know *et voilà.*

Happiness

As soon as I slept Poet rose up and stood over my body
he saw me weak & weird with metallic blue toenails tiny

toucan beaks that wanted to fly off into the universe made it
out of the window. I stretched out in a treetop to rest.

The stars were inquisitive eyes. I was plankton in a cave I was
a pack of lies I was being somewhere else I was finding

answers Poet craved. I woke up stranger to my body surrounded
by feather boas reindeer moss a handful of the afterlife.

I Won't if You Don't

At minus three minutes to my first breath when love was
the B&W noise of my mother's womb Poet died peacefully in

my sleep at fifty-two in a room on Elm's Avenue. At eighty-three
Poet died cradling my balls in a tepid bath on a morning that

lasted a hundred years. At twenty Poet died with the precision
of the Seoul Ryu Kyong Su 105 Guards Tank Division like an arsonist

stoking his chronic ashes Poet charred & died clearing through
boxes in the loft I found a note 'Don't die. I won't if you don't.'

Acknowledgements

Thanks are due to the editors of *Granta,
Oxford Poetry*, *Poetry Review*, *The Rialto*,
Shearsman and *Stand*, where early
versions of some of these poems appeared,
and to BBC Radio 4 Four Thought for
commissioning me to deliver a talk on the
poems in this collection. Warm thanks to
the Arts Council, Hosking Houses Trust and
Wellcome Trust for their support during
the writing of this book. I am grateful to
Simon Wragg for providing me with a room
of my own when it was most required.
I am indebted to the sharp eyes and
bright ideas of Jess Chandler, publisher
and sounding board, and Matthew Caley,
a meticulous editor. Most of all, I am
indebted to the many 'correspondences
in the air', as Anna Akhmatova
described the moments where poets of
different geographical and historical
circumstances, languages and traditions
address each other in their work.

@astridalben

About Prototype

poetry / prose / interdisciplinary projects /
anthologies

Creating new possibilities in the publishing
of fiction and poetry through a flexible,
interdisciplinary approach and the
production of unique and beautiful books.

Prototype is an independent publisher
working across genres and disciplines,
committed to discovering and sharing
work that exists outside the mainstream.

Each publication is unique in its form
and presentation, and the aesthetic of
each object is considered critical to its
production.

Prototype strives to increase audiences
for experimental writing, as the home for
writers and artists whose work requires a
creative vision not offered by mainstream
literary publishers.

In its current, evolving form, Prototype
consists of 4 strands of publications:
(type 1 // poetry) / (type 2 // prose) /
(type 3 // interdisciplinary projects) /
(type 4 // anthologies).